Book Description

Are you interested in Caribbea͏ the Arawakan people?

One of the indigenous tribes of the Caribbean, the Arawakans are a fascinating study in how culture and social order can be disrupted and wiped out by one historical event – the colonizers' arrival.

This account explores the Arawakan people and their culture in detail, together with an exploration of the events surrounding Christopher Columbus's arrival and what followed – the Arawakans were forced to change their social institutions and forget about their identifying culture, almost overnight. Analyzing these events enables us to understand the similarities between Arawakan and the modern Caribbean culture.

In this book, you will:

- Discover who the Arawakan people were
- Learn where they came from
- Explore their culture and social institutions
- Read in detail about the arrival of Christopher Columbus
- Learn about the devastating effect Columbus' arrival had on the Arawak
- See the differences between the Arawak and the Carib
- Investigate the Taino Rebellion
- Investigate how the Arawak genocide came about
- And so much more!

If Caribbean history is important to you or if you are a history enthusiast in general and want to learn more about these interesting people and their cultures, then this book is for you.

Click on the buy now button to get your copy of this book today and immerse yourself in the fascinating journey of the Arawak.

The Arawak

History of the Natives of the Caribbean Encountered by Christopher Columbus and Their Genocide

Table of Contents

Introduction

Chapter 1: Origin of the Arawak

Chapter 2: Culture of the Arawak

Chapter 3: Columbus and the First Encounter

Chapter 4: Slavery and the Holocaust

Bonus Chapter: Quick Guide to the Arawak

Conclusion

References

Introduction

Caribbean history is rich and varied, filled with fascinating stories, some even horrifying. You are about to embark on a journey of how the Caribbean islands first became inhabited, and how they became an important part of Christopher Columbus's voyage. We will focus on one small but critical part of history – the Arawak, an indigenous tribe of peaceful farmers who date back to pre-historic times. First, you will discover where they came from, what they did, and how they lived before you dive into the arrival of Columbus and his encounter with the Arawak.

The idea behind this book is to shed light on how the region's cultural landscape changed. The Arawakan genocide was a major historical event that changed the region's social atmosphere, and in this book you will gain detailed insight into the events that led to it. You will discover who the Arawakans were and learn about their culture before discussing Christopher Columbus and what happened when he discovered the tribe. You will uncover the events that followed, that eventually led to genocide, and the far-reaching effects – then and now.

Chapter 1: Origin of the Arawak

Picture this – more than 25000 years ago, the Bering Land Bridge brought about the first waves of migration onto American soil. Of those first migrations, around 5000 BCE Paleolithic Indians landed on the Caribbean, followed by Mesolithic Indians between 1000 BCE and 500 BCE. These tribes were known as the Ciboney; they settled in Haiti, Cuba, the Bahamas, and Jamaica, followed soon after by Neolithic Indian tribes known as the Kalinagos and Tainos. The latter covered quite a broad group, including the Tainos of the Greater Antilles, the Ignerians of Trinidad and Tobago, the Lucayans of the Bahamas, and the Borequinos of Puerto Rico. History suggests that most of these tribes would have entered the Caribbean through Trinidad, close to Venezuela, and canoes would have been used to ferry them over; from there, they began their migration to the Greater Antilles.

What's missing is any mention of the Caribs or the Arawaks, and that is quite significant in itself. The Arawak name was given by Europeans who interacted with the Lokonos and, today, it is used to designate a language. The original name is likely to have been provided by the Lokano, who inhabited a settlement in Aruacay, Orinoco. Friendly with the Spanish, the Lokonos freely traded and offered gifts to the Spanish, possibly as a way of intimating they were a peaceful people. This may well have resulted in their being spared from capture and slavery – at least to start with. According to legend, the Lokonos adopted Aracuas to indicate they were friendly, and that eventually became Arawak – the Caribbean's peaceful people. The Caribs were the third group to settle in the Caribbean, following the Arawak migration route but much later.

The Arawak were considered the most important group in the region because they were a much larger tribe than the other groups. In many ways, this makes it easier to study their culture, although not much is known about them before Columbus made landfall in the 1400s. We do know that they were largely a peaceful tribe, focused on farming and survival through the Caribbean, Guyana, and South America, specifically around the Andes.

Fighting did not come naturally to them, and they tended to be pushed around by other tribes, often being forced to relocate — one reason why little about their early days is known. This was also one reason why Columbus described them as "docile" when he wrote to King Ferdinand and Queen Isabella of Spain. He went on to say that they could be made to comply and give in to Spanish demands.

Antillian Arawak farming communities, sometimes containing 3000 or more people, were set up along rivers and on the coast where they could easily fish for their main source of food. They also grew 3 primary crops — tobacco, maize, and cassava, farming in a slash-and-burn manner of cultivation. The women were the workers, farming the land, cooking meals, and looking after the children while the men spent their days lying in hammocks, doing little. European sailors later adopted hammocks as beds, preferring them to the flea-infested straw they used to sleep on. We also know that the Arawaks were incredibly hygienic people, frequently bathing because, in their eyes, sweat harmed the soul. The Caribs forced them out of the area not long before the Spanish arrived on the scene.

South America Arawaks lived in the west and north of the Amazon basin in much smaller settlements. They were hunters and fishermen, sharing their livelihood with other tribes who inhabited the tropical forest, and with little to no hierarchical organization. We can also trace them to the west, to the Andes' foothills, where they were known as Campa Arawak, but these stayed isolated and largely unaffected by Andean influence.

It isn't easy to determine the spread of the Arawak population before Columbus arrived, and we can only use population growth models to estimate it. We know that Hispaniola Island is where more than 50% of the population lived, while the others inhabited St Lucia, Trinidad, Cuba, and Dominica. Their population distribution was still categorized as dense, due to the lack of adequate resources to support more people.

What I have been able to offer you here is just an overview of the Arawak people. In further chapters, we'll go into more detail about their culture before moving onto the crux of this book – the Spanish's arrival and their appalling treatment of the Arawak.

The accuracy of the figures in this book are wholly dependent on the original sources, like Christopher Columbus's written records, but it doesn't stop there. It also depends on how historical experts interpret the facts, and there are few sources unbiased enough to present anything close to an accurate view. One source that we can rely on, if only to a certain extent, is the US Library of Congress, and, using their records, we believe we have given you an accurate historical representation. You should still form your own opinions based on the information available, rather than believing one or another account of events.

Chapter 2: Culture of the Arawak

This chapter will look at the Arawakan culture, how they came to settle in the Caribbean, and how they survived for so long. The first part of the chapter deals with the "lingo," terms that you need to understand if you are to understand the people and their culture.

We'll also talk about the differences between the Arawak and the Carib, differences that you may not see at first glance.

The name "Arawak" was popularized by Europeans who colonized the land. This term encompasses all South Americans who identified as "Lokono" or "Aruhuco." The other name for the Arawak was "Taino," which meant "relatives." It could have been used to distinguish themselves from their relatives, the South American mainland Arawak people.

One of the biggest parts of any culture is the language because it is how we communicate at the end of the day. The Arawakan language appears to have originated within the South American river settlements, mostly those on the Orinoco river. Until the Europeans colonized America, Arawakan languages were the most prominent between the Orinoco and the Amazonian rivers and the new islands that would eventually be inhabited by the Arawak. So, by that, we can say that the 15th-century Caribbean tropical forest people originated from these river regions. It also means that the closest linguistic and ethnic relation of the Arawak in the modern world would be in communities residing in the tropical forest regions of South America. Examples of tropical forest populations closely related to the Arawak are the Chibcha, the Caracas, the Jirajira, and other ethnically similar populations.

The Arawak were skilled at working the land and had a couple of unique methods that left the evidence of their existence in the soil they once cultivated. Historians believe that the Arawak had ways to modify the soil to increase the productivity of the lands. One such method was adding charcoal to the land to make "black earth." This method increases the minerals in the land, thereby ensuring a more bountiful harvest. Along with using ash and charcoal, the Arawak also used feces to enrich the soil and increase its productivity.

This way is still popular today, and historians found evidence of the "black earth" method employed in the Caribbean. Another trait of the Arawak was abandoning the land that they were cultivating right after harvesting it. The land could not be cultivated all year round by the agricultural experts of that population, so it was abandoned after one harvest. The land was plucked and prodded with sticks making the mounds they needed for the seeds to be planted. Crops that they cultivated included cassava, sweet potatoes, beans, maize, and hot peppers. These became an essential part of their diet and are part of the modern Caribbean diet as well, meaning the genocide did not wipe out their culture altogether.

They also cultivated cotton and tobacco, two crops the Europeans showed interest in, along with the gold that could be seen adorning the locals as decorations. Tobacco was not only a great part of the entire social setting in that region but had intertwined itself with the religious ceremonies that they performed. It was an important commodity in the Europeans' eyes, who looked to make a great trade out of it.

Gold was another important concept in Arawakan communities, but we should first discuss more about their food sources. Farming gave them one outlet for producing food, but it wasn't their only source. Arawakan people also relied on fishing and hunting to supply the nutrients they needed, and there were quite a few species that they managed to catch. They regularly fished for turtles and lobsters by hand but employed baskets, hooks, nets, and spears to catch other, much larger species, such as sharks and large turtles. The Arawak also killed parrots, ducks, geese, iguanas, and small rodents to add to their food stores, as well as sloths, since they were in abundant supply. While a few of their food preferences, such as lobster and turtle, have survived to this day, the demand for sloth has not. In several places, they even used the maize they grew to make beer.

Because they had such a rich and varied source of protein, not to mention the crops they are in the fields, the Arawak people were healthy and well-fed; this lasted until immigrants arrived in what Columbus called "the new world." The increase in population, added to the import of new animal species, eventually resulting in famine. But it was how the Arawak's prepared their food that was unique to their culture and it has survived in today's culture still being featured in modern-day Caribbean food. They used plenty of spices and peppers grown within the region to give the food its trademark flavor. They also used these spices to help preserve their food. The women usually cooked the meats over either an open flame or on hot stones. These methods are still used in parts of the region nowadays, and it is fascinating to see that several well-known Caribbean dishes originated from this period.

One of the more interesting aspects of the Arawakan culture is gold, interesting because the islands were not particularly abundant in it. While it could have been part of the European agenda to locate and mine gold, there were no large deposits to be found. That said, the natives were skilled at mining what gold was there, but they didn't trade in it. Resources were so low that long-distance trading simply wasn't feasible in the same way it was for the European-discovered gold in West Africa. The Arawak mainly used gold for jewelry and decoration, which was confirmed by relics discovered over time.

The political/social system within the Arawakan community is of great interest to historians as well. Unlike anything the Europeans had seen, it had similarities that were overlooked since they were not evident to the naked eye. They lived in a theocratic system ruled by the gods they called "zemis." These "zemis" were represented by different objects that were usually in the village chief's possession. Such objects were made of stone, wood, and even human remains. They were presented to the population for worship, with the villagers offering beverages and bread to please the "zemis." The villagers believed that doing so would grant them protection from the wrath of the gods. They prayed for protection from floods, diseases, and other natural disasters.

The chief may seem unimportant in this system, but he was responsible for distributing resources and organizing food-gathering – fishing was allocated to the men while the women were responsible for crop cultivation and gathering. He was also responsible for settling disputes among his people and generally keeping the peace. The level of his importance was determined by the size of his subjects (number of people). It was also determined by the number of "zemis" he presented to the people. The people paid a small amount of tax to the chief for overlooking and protecting them. The chief also had assistants who were part of the common folk and not meant to receive a salary from the chief. Their positions in this social system were of honor, and they used this to receive services from the villagers.

Historians used this information to deduce the Arawakan social hierarchy and have agreed that the chief, in such populations, was prioritized and respected by the villagers. The villagers recognized the hierarchy and lived with a few differences between them and the chief. For example, the chief lived in a square hut, and the villagers lived in a circular hut. The chief was also responsible for the zemis and his importance, as discussed previously, is dependent upon the zemis he protects/brings. The religious belief of the Arawak revolved around this hierarchy where the nature spirits and zemis topped the charts, followed by the chief and then the commoners themselves.

From this, we can begin to piece together a more complex picture of the Arawak. We can see that they were peaceful, preferring to live in harmony instead of giving in to warfare. It's safe to say that they put a lot of effort towards trying to prevent it, using body paint (more on that later) and other techniques. Of the two primary tribes, the Carib were the more violent, as suggested by the fact that they drove the Arawak out of lesser Antilles before the Spanish arrival. Differences between the two groups are discussed in more detail in the next section.

The people in these settlements lived in huts built from wooden frames that were topped with straw. The huts had an earthen floor and an almost non-existent interior finishing. From this description, it may sound like these accommodations wouldn't hold up against mother nature, but for them to survive the climate in the Caribbean, they had to be tough, and they were! They were strong enough to resist hurricanes. Although, without more historical information experts are hesitant to make any further deductions.

Similarly, the beliefs and environmental factors had to weigh into what the locals wore. Their everyday attire is important to historians for the same reasons that their other cultural factors are important. The Arawak's attire consisted of scanty clothing made from cotton grown on their own plantations. The tropical climate rendered the locals almost naked during most of the year. The men were usually fully naked while the women wore a cloth to cover their genitals. This is not surprising information, but there was more to their wardrobe than just that. The single men and women were almost always naked, and the married women were required to wear an apron below their waist. This clothing allowed the chief to see how many women in his tribe were married and how many were not; indeed, those that were not married were not categorized as adults.

The Arawak also wore small ornaments of gold and sometimes shell too, often around the neck or the nose region. Wearing ear piercings of such ornaments was also a common trend. Gold was used in such ways rather than for trading purposes. The Arawak were also not interested in trade with the Europeans when they sought out precious commodities. The presence of such gold ornaments is a testament to the Arawakan art form.

The ornaments, as well as the pottery, reflected the creative influences of the people. The villagers decorated the pottery with motifs of birds and other animals that were part of the hunt. Usage of cotton for crafting hammocks and clothes was another form of expression that showed that the tribe was creative. Outside influences made them adapt and eventually take up western attire introduced by the colonizers.

Another common feature of the outfit is body paint. The Arawak painted their bodies in bright colors to serve cultural purposes. They believed that objects like rocks could be homes for evil spirits and so painted special patterns on their body to protect themselves from such spirits. They also wore amulets and gold ornaments for such reasons. They wore body paint to frighten and intimidate their opponent in battle, since warfare was also a common feature of the landscape. The wives often drew body paint during special rituals connected to zemi worship, as explained in this chapter. In this way, all social institutions influence one another in Caribbean society. The clothing/attire is influenced by religion, the chief, as well as the enemy.

Gold was the most prized possession of this settlement in terms of value in the modern world. The Arawak did not necessarily treat it as such because their values were quite different. Their most prized possession, instead of gold, was canoes. The Arawak could make canoes that carried more than fifty people at a time. Such vehicles were important since they suited the ecosystem of the smaller Caribbean islands. The Arawak used them for transportation and fishing activities. An academic can easily see why the canoes were more precious to the Arawak than the Europeans' gold.

Other possessions of the Arawak included stools, cloth, hammocks, wooden dishes and bowls, and gourds. The gourds were essential to carry drinking water, while the wooden dishes and bowls were essential for serving food. These bowls were also made of clay in certain areas, depending on the materials available to them. The hammocks were a luxurious item used for lounging around or sleeping. They have persisted the wrath of time, are still a part of the Caribbean culture, and they are frequently seen in many coastal cultures because of the ingenuity of the product itself. Other possessions can be found in many other sources related to the history of the region, but these were the most common articles found. The Arawakan even made beer from maize in this period, which has, of course, withstood the test of time.

The family's social institution was widely different from what it is today; the original institution was lost with the civilization. The turn to monogamy was a sign of colonization that contributed to the eventual imbalance created in the region. The Arawakan community usually had two to three wives who lived with them or lived with the children in a separate hut.

The activities for both the men and women were also different. The men were associated with the masculine norm and given activities that involved more strength, while the women were given activities associated with the feminine norm. These social and sexist norms did exist in society until the very recent and ongoing feminist movement that looks for equal opportunities for both genders. The men were supposed to hunt and provide for the community, while the women were responsible for cooking. The women of the tribe were also responsible for the agricultural side. They had to tend to crops and help out in the harvest. Another one of the wives' duties was to paint their husbands' bodies according to their rituals.

The Arawakan community was extremely strict about gender roles, and there was rarely any infringement of those unspoken social rules. The chief in these communities had more than two or three wives. In fact, marrying the chief was considered to have positive connotations since it came with status. The community had norms that made women have a sense of honor for marrying the village's chief. Historical reports estimate that the chiefs had more than thirty wives in many communities, making the family's modern institution an opposite and dystopian phenomenon.

Technologically the Arawakan population brought forward many great ideas, yet those ideas could not even come close to those introduced by the Europeans. The Arawakan deployed the stone making method to forge tools and the religious artifacts that they held so close to them. They could also use the stone-making technology to build houses, but the information collected from the rediscovered remains of huts tell us this did not truly occur. The huts barely used any stone at all, indicating that there might be a shortage of materials or skills required to produce a lot of stone structures. Weaving baskets was also a new idea introduced by them, painting over and carving pottery/ceramics.

The final topic that is part of the Arawakan life and culture is the way they defended themselves. As explained already, the Arawak were motivated to live a peaceful life and resented the idea of war. Therefore, they barely had any effective weaponry. The only weaponry they did possess was defending themselves against the violent group that chased them out of their lands. The Caribs were carnivores and needed to be fought off. The Arawak were experts at extracting poison from snakes and the bitter cassava as well. They used this poison on the tip of the arrows they used. It proved to be quite effective at keeping the Carib at bay. Along with that, they had a couple of fishing hooks attached at the end of rods and other similar makeshift weapons. All of these signs tell us that the Arawak were peace-loving humans working towards an afterlife that was suggested by their religion.

The Caribs were the other group that existed in the Caribbean region during the fifteenth century. They arrived shortly after the Arawak had completed their move to the Caribbean. The cultural practices of the Carib are like those of the Arawak, but there are a few social differences between the two groups.

They resided on the eastern islands and possessed similar canoes to the Arawak but used them for different purposes. As described, the Caribs were considered more violent, so the canoes were utilized for "warlike" purposes, adding to their far superior mobility. There were instances where the Carib abducted the

Arawakan women and married them. These women were responsible for raising the Carib children. Thus, the differences between the two cultures were blurred since many religious practices were passed on to the children. The Arawakan mothers of these children ensured that the religious practices were kept alive.

The social structure of the Carib society was also manufactured to reflect their mobile status. They were usually made up of small numbers. Each group was usually just one extended family that conducted raids on neighboring groups to obtain wives and other young ones' resources. This culture spread throughout the Carib society and reached the Arawak as well. Raids were conducted on Arawakan soil, which eventually drove the peace-loving tribe out of the region.

The stark difference between the two groups were that the Carib group were known to abduct and kill members of the Arawak population and carry out a ritual where they ate them. This cannibalism is what set them apart, but according to European reports, this may be a false statement about the Carib. European narrative do feature stories about the Carib's being the most feared tribe in the Caribbean. They were known as warriors, and the Europeans were smart enough to keep their distance in the beginning.

The Carib also faced different circumstances when the Europeans eventually settled. They survived the epidemic diseases at a better rate because of the small groups they had formed on the smaller islands. Both shared a similar fate in the end where most of their populations were wiped out due to events discussed in the next few chapters.

Chapter 3: Columbus and the First Encounter

Between 1492 and 1504, Christopher Columbus led four oceanic expeditions to America, a land unknown to the Old World (Africa, Europe, and Asia). This phase witnessed the colonization of these islands, the development of maritime trade across the Atlantic, and was ultimately highlighted as discovering the New World. Initially, Christopher Columbus wanted to search for westward oceanic routes to the Indies as, at that time, it was only accessible through arduous land routes. There was gold in Asia, and the spices and silks made a lucrative profit in Europe.

With the emergence of the Ottoman Empire, the Turks took control of Constantinople and controlled all the land routes that led to Asia. These circumstances presented the need for a sea route. Traveling west along the southern tip of Africa presented a viable solution, but it had never been done before. The Indies (East Indies) was known to be an extraordinarily rich hub of spices, gold, silver, pearls, and jewels. He wanted to bring with him the gold and spices from the Indies, where it was thought to be found in abundance, to benefit from their lucrative trade in Europe.

To prepare for this journey, he read the works of famous writers like Imago Mundi, a French cardinal; moreover, his expeditions were also partly inspired by the travels of a popular Italian explorer of the 13th century, Marco Polo. Due to this self-study, Columbus had developed certain convictions, among which several were set in falsehood and delusion. He thought Spain was closer to China towards the West than the East, so he thought he had reached the East Indies when he came across the American Islands. Columbus did not admit his failure despite the evidence.

This is the event why the islands of the Caribbean today are known as the West Indies.

For this voyage to the West, Columbus was accompanied by his crew that took three ships - the Santa Maria, Nina, and Pinta. They sailed from the Palos de la Frontera on the 3rd of August 1492 and reached the Canary Islands six days later. The broken rudders of the ship Pinta were repaired on the Island of Gran Canaria, and the outfitting of other ships were repaired. They departed on the 6th of September, and five weeks later, they founded the Indies. Triana (also known as Juan Bermejo), a sailor aboard, was first to sight the land and alert the rest of the crew. Later Columbus would claim that indeed, he was the first to sight land, which would win him a reward of 10,000 maravedis annually. They called this island San Salvador, but the natives of this land called it Guanahani. According to the modern world, it is the present-day island of the Bahamas or Turks and Caicos.

The following chapter will cover the first encounter and perceptions that Columbus had about the native people. The information is derived from his various letters and recorded testimonies that have been used by many historians. The Spanish's intentions, the Arawak's role in their mission of increasing their power through the New World's discovery and the treatment of Arawak after their encounter with Columbus are discussed. We will look at the distinguishing patterns in the natives' behaviors compared to the native Americans and the impact of the lust for gold in the mistreatment. By going over the accounts of a crucial witness, who have recorded these events and are credited by most historians as a credible source of information, the chapter debunks common misconceptions about gold's impact.

When they showed up on the Bahamian land, they were met by the native people of the land called Arawak, who swam up to them. These people lived in small communities within villages and grew corn, yam, and cassavas for agriculture. They could spin and weave but did not have any animals for work and they also did not have any iron for tools and weapons but wore ornaments made of gold in their ears. When the Spanish people came ashore with their swords, the Arawak greeted them with food, water, and gifts. Columbus dubbed these people *Indios*, Spanish for Indians, due to his false belief that he was in the East Indies. He described the people in various letters as "naked as the day they were born" because they wore very few clothes but wore gold. This told Columbus that the land he had found was rich in gold and jewels.

Slowly, Columbus started to take over all the islands that he came across, including Haiti, which he named Espanola, meaning Spanish Island. It was later Latinized and called Hispaniola. Columbus found these native people incredibly attractive; historians believe that they were the most handsome group of people he came across during his expeditions. They were built well and had great bodies.

Moreover, their nature was more beautiful than their physical characteristics. He described them as "people with such kind hearts and so ready to give the Christians all that they possess, and when the Christians arrive, they run at once to bring them everything." Columbus believed that they were like innocent people living peacefully without any laws, judges, or intuition.

On nearby islands, Columbus found native people who identified as Caribs. They conformed to the ancient picture of anthropophagi, something he had read about. According to the Arawak, their enemies, the Carib, were man-eaters who lived in the Lesser Antilles and surrounding Southern America. They greeted Europeans who approached them with poisoned arrows, which were shot in showers by both Carib men and women alike. Not only were these people more ferocious, but in comparison to the Arawak, they were more active and dynamic. The Spanish found them to be more civil than the Arawak, claiming that although their homes were made of straw, they were better constructed and had better supplies.

Columbus wanted to dominate these people for one reason – to use their labor to extract gold from the land and craft tools and weapons for the Spanish. His initial plan was to load ships with Caribs and send them over to Spain to learn their language and convert them from their cannibalistic ways. Later, the Spanish could exploit their dynamic skills and energetic behavior for manpower. This plan was to materialize by sending ships filled with cattle from Spain to the Caribbean, where they would assist in agriculture. In return, Columbus would send ships full of Carib men and women. This plan was never put into action due to disapproval from the Spanish authorities and the Carib people's successful resistance with their arrows. Instead, Columbus turned to the more peaceful, pliable Arawaks, people he thought would make great Christians.

On Christmas day in 1942, the Santa Maria - the biggest ship of Columbus' fleet - had to be scuttled during the expedition. At this point, the Spanish began their civilization of the Arawak people. The local Arawakan leaders of the island, dubbed Espanola, came to help Columbus' men to save everything that could be saved from the ship. Once again, Columbus described these people as "lacking greed" and "full of love." While this rescue mission was under process, canoes full of Arawak from other parts of the island came floating in. They brought with them heaps of gold to console the Spanish for their ship's loss, and Columbus repaid this act of kindness. He built a fortress on the same spot with an overarching tower and moat. The fortress was the first military base in the Western Hemisphere. He called it La Navidad, left behind thirty-nine of his men, and instructed them to direct their effort to find gold and store it.

This civilization process worsened, and the policies of terror became more intense after introducing a new system called the Encomienda. There was a cruel tribute system in the palace that required the locals to pay in gold or cotton. Despite being harsh, this system somewhat maintained the old social arrangements of the Arawak, being structured in such a manner that the old leaders were now under the control of the royal directions implemented through the viceroy.

With time as Spanish settlers started to arrive at the island, there was discontent with the current system. The Spanish settlers did not agree with the centralized method that was currently in place, and their actions completely disregarded it. They wanted a fair share of the Arawak's rich land and wanted to exploit the native people for labor and their human resources equally. Christopher Columbus' soon faced a revolt from these Spanish settlers when their demands were satisfied. In 1499 these revolts forced a discontinuation of the system that sought tribute through the centralized local chieftains and replaced it with a new one. The natives could be exploited through the new one, without any check on them from the central power. This system was called the encomienda's, and under it, the Spanish settlers were rewarded with the natives.

In theory, it was believed that the natives would benefit from this system, too, as they were introduced to the Christian belief. The implementation of this system was initially launched on a large scale in America, which led to Columbus losing his economic control over the region. This change impacted his authority as he was forced to step down, and a new governor for this newfound land was appointed by the monarchy back in Spain. This new system meant that the Arawak were forced to work more hours, often beyond exhaustion. They were also forced to convert to Christianity, which had been the Spanish mission - to 'introduce' Christianity. It was the introduction of the Encomienda system that hiked the mistreatment of the Arawak.

From the first time the Spanish set foot on the Caribbean's shores, they were hostile to the island's men. They were only invested in gold extraction, something that they had guaranteed the monarchs back home. It is recorded that after setting foot on the island, Columbus and his men asked the people about gold and immediately captured many of them in hopes that they would lead them to the site where gold would be found. Columbus' attitudes were motivated by the Spanish regime's promise that he would receive 10 percent of all the profits, the governorship of all the new land that he found, and the prestigious rank of Admiral of the Ocean Sea. This is why, despite finding the Arawak to be nice and gentle humans, he exploited them for their gold and personal and national gains.

Before leaving for Spain, the troops got into a fight because the Arawak refused to give them as many bows and arrows as they demanded. Two of the Arawak were slashed with a sword and left to bleed to death. This marked the inhumane treatment of the Arawak at the hands of the Spaniards.

Upon finding the West Indies (according to Columbus, it was the East Indies), Columbus returned to Spain to bear the news about Isabella and Ferdinand's discoveries. The monarchs were not as impressed with the findings of Columbus as much as he was. His account of his expedition in the court of Madrid was very extravagant when compared to reality. He defined Hispaniola as a land of "miracles," where there were wide rivers that were mostly filled with heaps of gold dust. He asked the Majesties for assistance, in return for bringing them most of this gold and as many slaves as they pleased. Spain was recently unified, and gold became a new measure of wealth across the New World and could be used to buy anything - even more important than the land that the Spanish monarchs controlled 95% of. The exaggerated reports and the knowledge and promise of gold convinced the Spanish regime to give Christopher Columbus seventeen ships and more than twelve hundred people.

After his return, he traveled from island to island, taking Indians captive. They were subjected to harsh labor, taken as sex slaves, and often beheaded if they refused orders. Many Arawak poisoned their babies and committed suicide to escape their fates. This eventually built up to the extinction of the entire Arawak population, discussed in detail in the following chapter.

Chapter 4: Slavery and the Holocaust

In the United States of America, Columbus is celebrated as a hero and remembered as the great explorer; he even has a national holiday dedicated to him, a way for the government to reassert the need to celebrate this historical figure. The romanticized account of his expeditions is popular within the masses. In contrast, the harsh reality is neither taught nor popularly known by the United States of America or the global populace. In reality, when Columbus arrived on the Caribbean islands like Hispaniola, he introduced very harsh policies that led to the gradual extinction of the land's indigenous people. His policies were cruel and genocidal, and they decimated a rich history of culture and race. Not only this, but Columbus was also a slave owner. One of his first thoughts, recorded in history when he met the Arawak was "that they would make good slaves".

In reality, his only intention was to set dominion over the native people to up his social standing in Spain's monarchical society. He chose to ignore the good nature of the Arawak, act on his lust for gold, and please the monarchy. He is known to have said:

"They have no arms and are all naked and without any knowledge of war, and very cowardly, so that a thousand of them would not face three. And they are also fitted to be ruled and to be set to work, to cultivate the land and to do all else that may be necessary, and you may build towns and teach them to go clothed and adopt our customs."

Once he was back from Spain, after bearing the news of his findings, he set on introducing these genocidal policies. From their newly established military base of La Navidad, Christopher Columbus sent new troops after troops into the island's interior to capture men and search for gold. More Arawak were being captivated and forced to bring them gold and jewels. There were various policies in place that stripped the Arawak of their human status and worked them tirelessly. A few of these policies are discussed in this chapter.

After arriving from Spain, Columbus built more forts and sent more and more slaves to Seville to benefit from the slave trade. As for the Arawak back on the island, they were being subjected to harsh policies in hopes to exploit the gold he believed existed there in abundance.

It soon became clear that Columbus was wrong, and there was not as much gold on the island as he had expected. Desperate to meet the promises made back in Spain and provide his investors with their fair dividend, he introduced a decree. According to this decree, all Arawak ages 14 or older were subjected to fill a hawk's bell full of gold every three months. Columbus made sure that this decree was in effect through the help of local leaders who were made responsible for supervising that all people fulfilled their quota. In places where there was no significant gold found, the quota could be replaced with twenty-five pounds of woven cotton, which would serve as a substitute for the gold dust.

When the local people met this quota, they were given copper tokens to hang around their necks. Those who did not meet the quota were not given a token and, if caught, would have their hands chopped off and be left to bleed to death. Unfortunately, there was not enough gold in the Espanola, and it was impossible to meet the Spanish target set. When the ship was scuttled, the pieces presented to Columbus resulted from years of accumulation that were now exhausted.

Sources also proclaim that he was presented with those pieces when he landed on the island. It was impossible to meet the targets, even after spending ridiculous hours on the riverbeds to sieve the gold dust out of it. As a result, many Arawakans tried to desert their fate by fleeing into the nearby mountains and hills. Sadly, they were hunted down by Columbus's men and slashed by swords, beheaded, or subjected to ferocious dogs trained to kill.

The only reliable source available today about what happened after Columbus set foot in the Caribbean are the accounts of Bartolome de las Casas, a young priest. He originally participated in the takeover of Cuba and, at one time, he owned slaves and plantations. After listening to a sermon, he gave his ways up and became a prominent critic of the Spanish practices. In particular, he was displeased with their cruelty towards the Indians. In one of his books called the *History of the Indies,* he writes that the Spanish were there to "ravage", 'kill", and "destroy". He suggests that every day was a new low, and Spanish would up the bar for being evil. At times, Spanish men would refuse to walk and would demand to ride on the backs of Arawak or be carried in hammocks when they were in a rush.

Moreover, the Indians were also forced to carry large leaves to protect the Europeans against the harsh, bright sun or fan them on a hot day. He also writes that there was no measure of accountability, and the Spanish men did as they pleased as there was no check on their power and actions. Knifing ten to twenty Arawak at once was not considered anything out of the ordinary, and the Spanish would slit the indigenous men and women open as they pleased just to check the sharpness of their blades. In one of the detailed accounts, Bartolome de las Casas writes how one day, the Spanish came across two boys carrying parrots of their own. Not only did the Spanish men rob the boys of their pets and take them away from them, but they also beheaded the boys for fun.

The men were subjected to harsh labor in the deep gold mines, and when men died, they had no one to turn to for help. They suffered the loss of their people in silence. It is said that around one-third of the men who worked in the mine lost their life due to harsh labor. To describe the exploitation of Arawak labor to the point of death, Bartolome de las Casas wrote:

"... mountains are stripped from top to bottom and bottom to top a thousand times; they dig, split rocks, move stones, and carry dirt on their backs to wash it in the rivers, while those who wash gold stay in the water all the time with their backs bent so constantly it breaks them; and when water invades the mines, the most arduous task of all is to dry the mines by scooping up pansful of water and throwing it up outside..."

The men were in these mines for around six to eight months, which was enough to melt the gold and meet their personal quota. While the men worked miles away in the mines, their wives were subjected to labor in the fields. They were forced to make countless hills for the cassava plants and work on the soil. The husbands and the wives barely got time to spend together, meeting perhaps once every eight or ten months and were extremely tired when they did. This meant that they did not have sex, as they were too tired for it. This hard labor also impacted the newborns as they were dying early due to both the parents working tirelessly. The overworked mothers did not eat well, and famine led to the mothers not making enough milk to feed their babies. According to Bartolome de las Casas, they also did not have time to nurse them, and therefore almost 7000 children died in Cuba. The husbands died extracting the gold, women died planting the cassava plant, and the newborns died due to the lack of milk. Due to these atrocities, the land that once housed more than a million Arawak was slowly starting to depopulate.

Burning captive Arawak slaves to secure heaps of gold, forcing them to overwork and travel long distances beyond the point of exhaustion, and sexually assaulting women and children to fulfill their lustful desires were just a few of the reasons contributing to the depopulation of the Arawak from America. One of the factors that is often ignored by many is the role of shock. Spaniards were there, in America, to conquer the land and they were overly aggressive and brutal in their approach to conquest.

There is no unanimous agreement on the statistic about how many Arawak were living on the Caribbean land when Columbus stepped foot on it. Some say a hundred thousand, a million, eight million, and others an entirely different number. Although if we were to believe that there were half a million Arawak, then the ratio of Spanish to Arawak men was 1:167. Although the advanced technology and weaponry that the Europeans had in their possession made up for this number. This meant that the Arawak could not compete with the Spaniards, their warhorses, and war dogs despite their human resources.

Additionally, the extreme manner the Spaniards used to deploy their weapons was done right from the start, shocking a native community who had never been faced with anything like this before. Eventually, this led to the Arawak people submitting to gradual defeat by the Spanish. Added to this was the introduction of the encomienda system, which led to a sharp rise in abuse against the native Arawak people. The natives could not fight against an armed and developed force of conquerors, leading to the collapse of their social group. Mothers even turned to infanticide to stop their children become slaves to the Europeans.

The women also saw how the men were treated brutally, many being killed, and chose infanticide to escape painful death. They didn't stop there, though. Seeing what was coming, they began to destroy their crops, in the hope that the resulting famine would drive the Spaniards away. Sadly, that didn't happen; instead, starvation set in, wiping out even more of the local people.

Perhaps one of the worst things to happen was the introduction of new diseases, brought to the New World by the Spanish. The Arawak did not have immunity to these diseases like the Old-World People did and, consequently, they began to die. There are many people who don't believe that disease was responsible for the Arawak depopulation but, with new evidence emerging, it appears that historians now think it did, in fact, play a crucial role.

According to written records, Columbus is said to have taken 9 Arawak men with him back to Spain to show the monarchs what he had found. It is believed that most of these men died during the journey, with many saying they died on the way to Spain and others saying it was on the way back. From the time Columbus set foot on the Caribbean islands, disease began to spread at an angry pace. Given the amount of time that has passed, and the lack of any real written evidence, it is extremely difficult to predict the diseases accurately. They mainly became widespread along Hispaniola since it was the epicenter of all the Spanish settlements.

That's not to say that the Caribbean islands did not have any diseases of their own. Both the Spanish and the Arawak lost lives, but most Arawak could not recover from the disease, while most Spanish had stronger physical strength and immunity. Many believe that diseases like leishmaniasis, Chagas disease, and tuberculosis were present on the island, which also weakened the natives and gave pace to their death. The Spaniards also brought typhus, cholera, smallpox, and malaria to the Islands, four diseases that the Arawak could not fight against.

Chanca was a surgeon and physician appointed to Columbus's men by the Council of Seville. Often, interpreters were used between the Spanish and the Arawak chief, but they were not effective at communicating symptoms. This led to Chanca not being able to help them, potentially leading to more unnecessary deaths. According to the Spanish monarchy's orders, and detailed in his appointment letter, Chanca's duties were to look after the Europeans, not the Arawak, or any other native on the islands. We can deduce, from what written records do exist, that the symptoms described suggest smallpox.

Many historians agree that smallpox was present in many European countries during that time, and others believe that the diseases were brought into the Caribbean through the African slaves imported to the Spanish estates illegally. In 1517, a maximum of 4000 slaves was allowed to be imported every year. The slave trade in the parts of Santo Domingo was supposed to be reserved for Spanish slave traders, but seeing the surge in demand, many Genoese and Portuguese traders capitalized on the opportunity and directly brought African slaves from West Africa. There are accounts known to us that vividly indicate that many of these slaves were sick and brought the disease with them when they arrived in America.

Within a matter of years, the Arawak population was wiped out. The diseases began to spread fast, killing large numbers of people, and those who survived killed themselves or were brutally murdered by the Spanish for reasons they seemed fit. Historians use the word genocide as these people who were the rightful owners of the land now cease to exist.

The Arawak suffered badly at the hands of the Spanish in their homeland but, despite outnumbering the Spaniards, they could not stage a successful resistance. Individual people tried to stand up to Columbus's tyrannical regime, but due to the Spanish weapons' superior might, they were shut down easily.

In 1511, the Arawak fought back against the Spanish in an effort known as the Spanish-Taino War or the Taino Rebellion.

When the Arawak chief, Agueybana I, the man who brokered the original peace deal with the Spanish, he was replaced by Ageuybana II. He began his reign as the unpopular encomienda system was brought in and was responsible for organizing several caciques, local leaders of the island's southern territories like Jumaco, Guyana, and more, and declared war on the Spaniards. One of the first attacks from this group of Arawak was on a Spanish officer of a high-rank, Diego Salcedo. He was murdered, and his settlement on the island was burned to the ground. After this attack, the war gradually progressed in stages. By 1513, the rebellion was over and the Spaniards, led by Ponce de Leon, won. Various Spanish commanders led incursions into the villages of various caciques, killing them and taking their men as slaves. In total, there were around 18 attacks carried out by the Spaniards on the Arawak, with regions like Otoao, Humacao, and Guyana attacked one after another.

As a response, and due to the lack of advanced machinery and war animals, the natives resorted to guerrilla tactics. They were on the move constantly throughout the process of their offensives and were using canoes to circle in the areas of San Juan. They also launched a counter-offensive from Daguao and attacked the capital of the Spaniards - Caparra. These attacks from Arawak were carried out through the 1520s and finally came to an end in 1529.

It all started when Juan Cerón, a representative to the Spanish viceroy, asked Agüeybaná II to assign Sotomayor, a high-ranking officer amongst the Spaniards, 40 natives to work in his villa, but request was not fulfilled as there was no compliance from the region's respected caciques. As a result, the Arawak people were brought in from the surrounding areas. But Sotomayor was not happy with the Spaniards' inability to enforce a large native workforce, so he ordered them to penetrate the settlements of the native and boost his troop of slaves. The Arawak fought back in defense of this aggressive behavior and attacked the Spaniards, causing them great injuries.

Then in 1509, the area originally designated for the Spanish by the Arawak chief was deemed too inhospitable, forcing a move to an area nearer the river. The Arawak decided to launch an attack on Sotomayor, who had now been appointed as a Chief Marshall. Sotomayor learned of the attack and decided to move out of Caparra, assisted by the guides and carriers supplied by the Spanish monarchs. However, the Arawak tracked Sotomayor and executed him near the Jauch river, which can be found in modern-day Jayuya.

Sotomayor was succeeded by Juan Gil Calderon, an active slave owner who had recently received 150 native Arawak from one of Agueybana's subjects. At the time, the Spanish were engaged in active battles with the natives, with Ponce de Leon leading the first one in 1511. He informed the Spanish Monarchy of the rebellion at the river now known as Descalabrado and was told to try to calm the situation. Part of the orders stated that the Spaniards should do whatever was considered necessary to suppress the rebellion, and that included using well-trained, armed men. The monarchy even allowed the use of local Spanish laws in the trails of the caciques. All tools and modes of transport that could be used to spark a rebellion were snatched from the natives, including their canoes. Anyone who failed to surrender to the Spaniards was considered an enemy of the monarchy, and war was declared against them. The hope was that this would deter others from joining the rebellion, forcing them to accept the peace settlement. And the leaders of those who failed to surrender were sent to the gold mines as slaves, hoping that it would deter others.

The San Juan Arawak used their canoes to attack the Spaniards, and this was when Ponce de Leon was brought in to put a stop to it. Agueybana's people were in contact with the Arawak rebel groups in Hispaniola and the Lesser Antilles by way of canoes. Later, when Alonso took power, the conflict continued. Ceron ordered an attack on Alonso's lands in 1512 and, a few days later, Agueybana's lands were attacked by Spaniards on horseback. All captured slaves were then sent to Villa San German to be auctioned.

In 1513, Spanish settlers' inflow increased in the Caribbean, partly because of an increase in gold deposits discovered in Loquillo. With wars abroad and few men to assist due to America's rebellion, the focus again moved to employ Arawak as workers. In hopes of ending the war, the encomienda system was abolished and replaced with one that allowed for an unsanctioned form of slave trading. This was used as a reason to target the Arawak by claiming their involvement in the war, especially those belonging to the Lesser Antilles. They were particularly targeted because, despite the equal involvement of Caribs in the rebellion, none of the captured caciques were identified as belonging to that race. Countless Arawak caciques were targeted and killed during this phase. Their children were also removed by justifying it through religious arguments, which stopped the line of succession.

Agüeybana II still had command over an army of 2000 Arawak. Similarly, eight caciques with their troops of around 350 people launched a counter-offensive that burned down a Spanish settlement, killing 18 Spanish men. Around 30 buildings were destroyed, and Agüeybana II was involved in the attacks himself. Some caciques resolved to destroy the Spanish settlement terrain and killed their livestock to damage their resources of survival. Reacting to the destruction caused by the counter-offensive of the natives, the Spanish deployed reinforcement of manpower to protect the settlers. A new headquarter was constructed near the base of the enemy, and widespread attacks were carried out from there on the local Arawak. Various caciques from different regions like Guayervas, Cayey, Guayama, and many more were detained on suspicion of their involvement in the rebellion and were deported to Hispaniola to restrict further involvement. Moreover, a widespread massacre was carried out in the Daguao and Virgen Gorda's regions, following incursions in Orocobix, Daguao, and Guaranty.

The Spanish front incursions continued until 1514, and their efforts focused on extracting gold from the Cordillera Central and squashing any rebels or organized resistance against their rule. The already compromised land was further stabilized by the arrival of African slaves into the region, all part of the Viceroy's plan to boost the Spanish workforce. Despite the attack on the Arawak, many stayed belligerent, refusing to accept peace. They continued attacking and inflicting damage on the Spanish, in the hopes of eventually escaping their tyranny, killing the Spanish until 1517.

The last report of an Arawak as chief was in 1518, after which the records about the further succession disappeared. With time the power of the Arawak decreased, as their numbers decreased. In 1518 the Spanish planned an attack to capture a high-ranking native who was part of the cause of the rebellions. The prisoner called himself "Cristóbal," a possible allusion to Agüeybana II. After Cristóbal's death, all records of the Arawak seem to have disappeared and, 20 years after the rebellion started, it ended, and the Arawak population were all but gone.

According to Diego Columbus's testimonies, the population of the native Arawak reduced from 60,000 to 33,000 between 1508 and 1510. The number further decreased to around 2,000 in 1519, and by 1542 there were no remaining Arawak on the island.

Bonus Chapter: Quick Guide to the Arawak

How is "Arawak" Pronounced and What Does it Mean?

It is pronounced "Air-a-wack" and is sometimes spelled as Arowak, Arawac, Aruak, or Arahuaco. It is the tribal name they gave to themselves and is derived from their primary crop – the cassava root or manioc. Many Arawak people called themselves "Lokono," which translates to "the people."

Where do the Arawak Live?

They are the original people of the Caribbean islands and northern regions of South America. Contrary to popular belief, they did not die out completely and descendants can still be found today in parts of French Guiana, Guyana, Trinidad, Suriname and parts of Northern Venezuelan coastal areas.

Are the Arawak the Same as the Guajiro and Taino People?

Not really. They are kin, their languages are related and many of their cultures are similar. All of them are collectively known as Arawakan but they are ethnically and politically separate. The Tainos natively inhabited Puerto Rico, the Dominican Republic, Cuba, Haiti, and Jamaica and descendants can still be found in those areas today. The Guajiros, also called the Wayuu, are naïve to Colombia and Venezuela.

Who Did Christopher Columbus Encounter – Arawak or Taino?

Primarily, the Taino but he did land on the Bahamas, important islands for indigenous trading and home to different tribes. That included the Carib and the Arawak.

Did Columbus Wipe Out the Arawak?

No. Although almost all inhabitants of the Bahamas were killed or enslaved by European colonists, other Arawak communities lived in other areas that didn't come under attack. Today, there are about 10,000 Arawak people and over half a million from related cultures, like the Guajiro.

What Language Do They Speak?

Most speak their own language, Arawak or Lokono but many also speak French, Spanish, Italian, or Dutch, depending on where their community is located.

How Were Arawak Indian Nations Organized?

They didn't have any form of central government; instead, each community had their own leader, called a chief or cacique. These were usually the previous chief's nephew or son, but some communities used religious leaders to choose their new chief.

How Did the Arawak Indian Children Live? What Did They Do?

The same way as kids of today do – they played together, learned lessons, helped in and round the house and the community. They were also taught to swim much earlier than European children. They didn't have formal schooling and were home-schooled by grandparents or village elders but, today, they attend school, the same as other kids.

What Were Their Homes Like?

Traditionally, they lived in thatched huts. Their climate was warm so there was no need for insulation and their huts were mainly to provide shelter from the rain and privacy. The huts were circular wooden frames covered in palm fronds, straw and woven mats. Their beds were woven hammocks hung from the hut frame. In many areas, huts like these are still used by the Arawak but most do live in more modern housing – the hammocks are still popular for sleeping in the existing villages.

What Was Their Clothing Like?

They didn't really wear much in the way of clothes – the weather was very warm and there wasn't considered a need. The men were naked, only wearing cloaks and loincloths for special occasions. The women were dressed in short skirts and wore shell necklaces. Typically, they went barefoot, and shirts or top coverings were not considered necessary.

They also did not wear headdresses, like the Sioux Indians did. Their hair was long – men and women – and they would sometimes have parrot feathers in it. In several communities, flower crowns were worn for festivals and body paint was used for festivals and battle.

What Was Their Primary Form of Transportation?

The Arawak typically used dugout canoes they built themselves. The word, "canoe" that we use today is derived from "canoa," the word used by the Arawak. The biggest canoes held up to fifty people and could be used for long-distance travel.

What Did They Eat?

The Arawak were a community of farmers, growing cassava, beans, peppers, squash, peanuts and corn. The cassava was ground into meal by the Arawak women and baked into bread. The men fished for turtles, fish and other seafood while hunters shot small game and birds.

What Were Their Tools and Weapons Like?

Hunters traditionally used blowguns or bows and arrows. Nets and traps built of wood were used by fishermen. Bows and arrows were typically used in warfare although hand-to-hand combat was also popular, using heavy wooden clubs.

What Were Their Crafts and Arts Like?

Arawakans were known for intricate woodcarvings and pottery.

Did They Interact with Other Native Americans?

They carried out frequent trade with different tribes, traveling the South American and Caribbean coast, carrying their goods for trade. The Guajiros and Taino were their most common trading partners, and they did trade, at times, peacefully with the Carib — when the Carib weren't attacking them and kidnapping villagers for slaves.

What Stories are Told by Arawak Indians?

Arawak people have many traditional fairy tales and legends, and it is an important part of their culture.

And Their Religion?

Religion and spirituality were an important part of life and many people still practice the traditional beliefs to this day.

Conclusion

This account's conclusion links all the stories and analysis in the other chapters with the present day and age. This chapter will enable the readers to understand the implications of all the events that have been explained in the chapters above. The Caribbean region did not just withstand the implications, but the entire world was somehow affected by the Arawakan settlement in the Caribbean region.

The major impact of the conquest is also the most obvious one. It is the loss of culture and tradition that has hurt the region the most. The identity and the region's rich culture have mingled with the western elements to form a new culture. This does not mean that the new culture is not bad, but the unique culture of the Arawak is still a loss to humanity. The peace-loving tranquil people have been rearranged in a frantic capitalistic system that is bound to create individuals rather than groups like there were in the fifteenth century.

The loss of life in that region also created a massive imbalance allowing other ethnicities to thrive. The native ethnicity declined in huge numbers while other ethnicities thrived in what was once a paradise for them. This loss of life is also a huge negative impact that can help people learn more about conquests. This pattern is observed throughout history. Whenever a crusade occurs, either the crusader is killed, or the natives are taken over. This means that the resultant feeling is always of loss. Therefore, nations' sovereignty is an important phenomenon that has come about post-world war I. Academics and other individuals must recognize that it was events like the Spanish crusade that led the world to evolve into the world's current political systems today. Other similar deductions can be made from this event. Some of them are explained in this section. This evolution can be considered positive depending on individuals' personal opinions on the political systems that exist in the world today. This can also be considered a negative implication since, without the Spanish crusade, the region's social system might not have changed at all.

Loss of diversity was one of the resulting losses from this conquest. Even though the spread of society's epidemics and reconstruction are re-explained as positive implications, the loss of diversity cannot be explained in such a way. This is one of the losses that cannot teach the lesson to the world since the race lost cannot be recovered. The loss of the Arawakan population meant losing a language and a certain lifestyle that was unique to the region.

The massive damage that was delivered to the land should also be categorized as a huge loss from that era. A lot of the land was eroded and overworked by the wars. The cultivation that was conducted by the Europeans for trade also affected the land negatively. This mass production and violence conducted on the Caribbean islands contributed to much of the pollution during the colonization period. The defensive wars that the Arawak were forced to partake in may have made massive changes to the landscape. There might have existed beautiful landscapes that we may never get to see because the war or the capitalistic machine destroyed them.

There are plenty more negatives that an individual or an expert can think of, but that is not the point. The point is understanding the substantial effect of the entire situation and the massive domino effect that this genocide has on the future generations of the region. The poverty and struggle future generations had to go through because of this genocide was also part of the domino effect. The dwindling numbers of the Arawak population meant that more work had to be taken by fewer numbers, putting more pressure on the already declining population. The domino effect as a whole can be considered as a huge negative implication of the Spanish crusade.

There are a few lessons that the world has learned from the crusade and the eventual genocide of the Arawak so that no one would repeat that era's actions. These lessons are, therefore, included in the positive section of this chapter.

The first positive lesson can be learned from the spread of disease. This was the first step to creating a more integrated world, and the spread of disease from one place to another is always a threat. Ways to curb this threat should have been present, but this was unknown during the fifteenth century, so no one could come up with a way to tackle it. In the modern world, no one can travel without health cards and vaccine cards. Such an integrated system allows one place to be free of disease that may exist in another part of the world. This lesson does not mean that the disease's loss has been invalidated; in fact, the deaths from those diseases made this threat evident to the world. The most recent COVID outbreak shows how the world has not fully grasped this lesson and that the instruments that the governments are working with need to be upgraded to cater to the growing population numbers. The COVID pandemic example also shows how history is an important subject in terms of understanding mankind's mistakes and not repeating them. Sadly, those mistakes were repeated!

Another positive that can be taken from this Spanish conquest is that it initiated a new world. A world that we now know as the "global village" was initiated during the conquest. The entire trade system that the Europeans installed allowed all the different parts of the world to be connected. Each shared the mutual gains of the other. For example, tobacco grown in the Caribbean was enjoyed by consumers in the European world and vice versa. This is the global model that we live in today, and it seemed to originate through the colonization of the Caribbean islands.

Another positive impact was the byproduct of the two cultures intermingling. Many words from the Arawak Languages were adopted into the Spanish language. The Spanish language is officially the second language of most Caribbean regions and shows how these acts originated from. The history of a place is important to understanding and appreciating its current state. The current state of the Caribbean can be linked to the events described in this book. This will allow readers to finally get the big picture of the region so that they can put all the pieces together.

No matter how you interpret these events, the facts will not change. The facts have been presented as truthfully as possible. It is now up to the readers to grasp the intensity of the events and critically evaluate them.

"The Arawak" is the most complete and unbiased account of the events that took place in the fifteenth century and those that followed the initial encounter of the Arawak with Christopher Columbus. It is important to cover all the bases before reading about the encounter, so the first few chapters have done exactly that. The first chapter has been used to give out complete information about the lifestyle, nature, social institutions, and ambitions of the Arawak and its neighboring community, the Carib. That information alone is fascinating; however, reading about the initial encounter and the events that followed will give the readers a complete picture of the region's history. The last chapter completes this picture by providing a link to the modern era and the past. Many popular modern examples have been utilized to explain the analysis drawn from the events of the genocide.

The most important thing to do when reading about history is to be critically open about everything. Each fact should be met with both criticism and acceptance, since these were the views of our ancestors. This is what makes history a fascinating topic that can be understood by only a few.

I hope you enjoyed reading this book. If you did Consider leaving your feedback on amazon. Thank you

References

britannica.com. Arawak. n.d. Website, electronic. 11 01 2021.
<https://www.britannica.com/topic/Arawak>.

carriacou.biz. History of the Arawak Amerindians, Taino religion technology
and culture. n.d. Website, Electronic. 11 01 2021.
<https://carriacou.biz/arawaks-amerindians/>.

history.com editors. Spanish-American War. 14 05 2010. Website, electronic.
11 01 2021. <https://www.history.com/topics/early-20th-century-
us/spanish-american-war>.

Morgan, Edmund S. Columbus' Confusion About the New World. 10 2009.
Electronic, Website. 11 01 2021.
<https://www.smithsonianmag.com/travel/columbus-confusion-about-the-
new-world-140132422/>.

Richard Bulliet, Pamela Crossley. "The Earth and Its Peoples Fifth edition ."
Bulliet, Richard. Cengage Advantage Books, n.d.

Study.com. Arawak Peoples: Culture, Art & Religion. n.d.
<https://study.com/academy/lesson/arawak-peoples-culture-art-
religion.html>.

US Library of Congress. HISTORICAL AND CULTURAL SETTING. n.d.
Electronic. <http://countrystudies.us/caribbean-islands/5.htm>.

Printed in Great Britain
by Amazon

23110165R00030